Men's Hats

IL CAPELLO DA UOMO

Adele Campione

CHRONICLE BOOKS

SAN FRANCISCO

First published in the United States of America by Chronicle Books in 1995.
Copyright © 1988 by BE-MA Editrice.

Printed in Hong Kong.

Library of Congress Cataloging-in-Publication Data:
Campione, Adele.
   [Cappello da uomo. English & Italian]
   Men's Hats = Il Cappello da uomo/Adele Campione;
   [caption translation, Joe McClinton; photography, Cesare Gualdoni].
      p.   cm.— (Bella cosa library)
   English and Italian.
   Originally published: Italy: BE-MA Editrice, 1988.
   ISBN 0-8118-1059-3 (pb)
   1. Hats. I. Title II. Title: Cappello da uomo.   III. Series.
   GT2110.C3513   1995
   391'.43—dc20   94-43850
                                                CIP

Caption translation: Joe McClinton
Photography: Cesare Gualdoni
Series design: Dana Shields, CKS Partners, Inc.
Design/Production: Robin Whiteside

Distributed in Canada by Raincoast Books
8680 Cambie Street
Vancouver, B.C. V6P 6M9

10 9 8 7 6 5 4 3 2 1

Chronicle Books
275 Fifth Street
San Francisco, California 94103

Men's Hats

*B*ecause of its position on the highest part of the body, the hat has always been both a useful protective accessory and a mark of identification among men.

Our selection of hats begins at the end of the fourteenth century and ends around 1950. We've chosen hats that are of special interest for their shapes and materials, their historical period, and the country in which they were worn. We will discuss the role of men's hats in the history of fashion and costume, as well as the symbolism that various hats were meant to express.

Handsome color photographs highlight the details that allow us to classify hats by period, country, social class, occasions of wear, level of power, and many other categories. This enjoyable voyage, filled with curiosities and anecdotes, will provide a stimulating look at 650 years of the history of fashion.

A high-crowned hat with a raised brim ending in a point, worn by noblewomen and knights, especially when traveling. It is identical to the *goliardo* worn by Italian university students at the beginning of the academic year and on festive occasions up until 1950 (Alessandria Museum).

Cappello a cupola alta, tese rialzate e terminanti a punta portato da dame e cavalieri soprattutto in viaggio. E' identico al goliardo, portato dagli universitari all'apertura del l'anno accademico e alle feste fino a tutto il 1950 (Museo di Alessandria).

A Spanish hat with a high, rounded crown and a wide brim, decorated with plumes and a silver buckle (Alessandria Museum).

Cappello spagnolo a cupola alta tondeggiante e a tesa larga; piumato e ornato da una fibbia d'argento (Museo di Alessandria).

A black felt hat with a tall, tapering crown, a black velvet band, and a silver buckle. This was the hat of the English Puritans and the Pilgrims who arrived in America on the *Mayflower* in 1620 (Alessandria Museum).

Cappello di feltro nero con cupola alta a tronco di cono, cinta in velluto nero e fibbia d'argento. E' il cappello dei puritani inglesi e dei Pilgrim Fathers sbarcati nel 1620 dalla Mayflower in America (Museo di Alessandria).

$\mathcal{A}$ black felt Louis XIV tricorne, ornamented with gold braid and an ostrich feather. This type of hat was the least likely to disarrange the enormous, stiffly curled wigs favored by the Sun King (Alessandria Museum).

Tricorno in feltro nero Louis XIV ornato da un gallone dorato e da una piuma di struzzo. E' il cappello che meno scompiglia le monumentali parrucche a boccoli rigidi predilette dal Re Sole (Museo di Alessandria).

A black felt Louis XV tricorne with gold braid and an ostrich feather draped over the turned-up brim. It was worn firmly pressed down on the forehead; by this time the white or silvery-gray wigs had become much smaller (Alessandria Museum).

Tricorno Louis XV in feltro nero, gallone dorato e piuma di struzzo ricadente oltre la tesa rialzata. Lo si porta ben calzato sulla fronte: ormai la parrucca, bianca o argentata, è di dimensioni ridotte (Museo di Alessandria).

$\mathscr{A}$ reddish-colored tricorne, edged with grosgrain ribbon of the same color and ornamented on the side with a pearl-centered cockade (Alessandria Museum).

Tricorno rossiccio bordato con canneté in tinta e ornato di lato da coccarda con perla centrale (Museo di Alessandria).

A beige felt Directoire cocked hat, or bicorne, ornamented with silk gros-grain ribbons and a mother-of-pearl button. The cocked hat was the hat of the new regime; for ceremonial dress, it was richly ornamented and plumed. This was also the hat worn by Napoleon (Alessandria Museum).

Bicorno Direttorio in feltro beige ornato di nastri in canneté di seta e da un bottone di madreperla. Il bicorno è il cappello del nuovo regime; nella tenuta da cerimonia, è riccamente ornato e piumato. E' anche il cappello di Napoleone (Museo di Alessandria).

A "half-stovepipe" of dove-gray felt, with silk brim edging and band, and a brass buckle at the side. The top hat, officially born at the end of the eighteenth century, was worn by aristocrats and other persons of privilege. But later, with a tapered crown, it became synonymous with revolution, like the cylindrical hat with a tricolor cockade worn by French revolution-aries (Alessandria Museum).

Mezza tuba in feltro tortora, bordo e cinta in seta e fibbia laterale di ottone. Il cilindro, o tuba, nasce ufficialmente sul finire del 1700, portato da aristocratici e persone facoltose. Ma poi, a cupola quasi conica, diviene sinonimo di rivoluzione sulla scia del cilindro con coccarda tricolore portato dai rivoluzionari francesi (Museo di Alessandria).

𝒜 "Calabrese," or Calabrian, hat. When the top hat took on a revolutionary symbolism, it evolved into a soft hat like this one, with a tall, tapered crown that recalls its origins in the French Revolution. Worn together with a velvet jacket with a red top pocket, the Calabrese became part of the typical revolutionary's outfit during the Italian Risorgimento (Alessandria Museum).

Cappello "calabrese". Divenuto reazionario, il cilindro cede il posto, oltre che al cappello floscio, a questo tipo di cappello che, a cupola alta a cono tronco, ne ricorda la funzione originariamente rivoluzionaria. In epoca risorgimentale, portato con giacca di velluto dal taschino rosso il cappello calabrese fa parte del tipico abbigliamento da rivoluzionario (Museo di Alessandria).

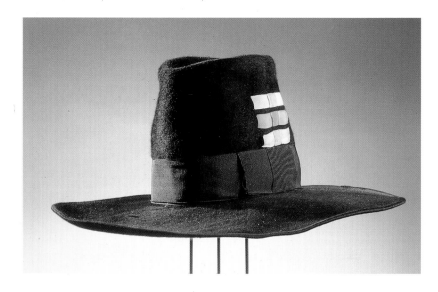

$\mathcal{B}$orsalino models from 1882, 1896, 1897, 1900, and 1903 (from *Omaggio al Capello*).

Modelli Borsalino 1882, 1896, 1897, 1900 e 1903 (da "Omaggio al Cappello").

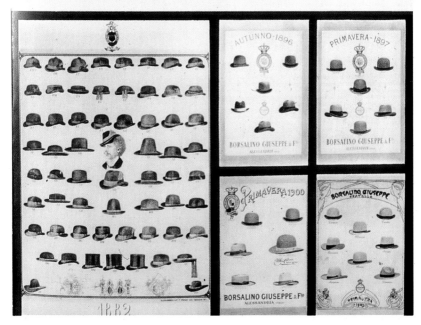

$\mathcal{A}$ tobacco-colored Borsalino, with edging on the outer side of the brim and a wide band, both of matching silk grosgrain. Giuseppe Borsalino went to France to learn hat making. On his return to Italy, he set up shop; the first hat came out of his factory on April 4, 1857. By 1875 his catalog listed sixty different models (Alessandria Museum).

Cappello Borsalino color tabacco, bordo fuori e cinta alta in canneté di seta in tinta. Giuseppe Borsalino va in Francia per imparare a fare il cappellaio. Rientrato in Italia, Borsalino si mette in proprio; il primo cappello esce dalla sua fabbrica il 4 aprile 1857. Nel catalogo del 1875 i modelli sono ormai 60 (Museo di Alessandria).

A bowler, or derby, of black shorn felt, with a black silk inner-brim edging and band (Mutinelli Collection). In Italy, the top hat was also known as the "pipe," the "ten-liter hat," or the "bomb." The bowler, or *bombetta* ("little bomb"), is indeed a lesser version of the top hat, both literally and figuratively. The bowler's crown is lower and more rounded than that of the top hat, and, unlike the top hat, the bowler was a hat for the masses.

Bombetta in feltro nero rasato, bordo in dentro e cinta di seta nera (Collezione Mutinelli). Il cilindro, oltre che tuba e decalitro, era anche chiamato bomba. Bombetta ne è il diminutivo in tutti i sensi; prima di tutto in senso letterale, e poi formale: la cupola si abbassa e si arrotonda, e poi sociale: è il cappello di tutti.

$\mathcal{A}$ black top hat with a "beaver" finish and a silk grosgrain edging and band. It was made in Monza, a center for the production of hats and caps since the Middle Ages and one of the first Italian cities to introduce mechanization. Monza was also famous for its "camel's-hair" top hats. Since mid-century, in Lombardy the top hat had been the symbol of the pro-Austrian sympathizer, with notable exceptions: The fervent Italian nationalist Giuseppe Verdi wore a top hat during the period of his "subversive" opera *Nabucco*, and also for his portrait by Boldini (Monza Museum).

Cilindro nero a pelo lungo, bordo e cinta in canneté di seta. Prodotto a Monza, produttrice fin dal Medio Evo di cappelli e berretti è tra le prime città italiane a introdurre il lavoro meccanico. Per quanto riguarda i cilindri, Monza era famosa per quelli di "pelo di gambello". In Lombardia, a partire da metà secolo il cilindro è sinonimo di austriacante, con le dovute eccezioni: Verdi lo porta in testa ai tempi del "sovversivo Nabucco" e nel ritratto del Boldini (Museo di Monza).

$\mathcal{A}$ light gray hat with a matching gray outer-brim edging, a black band, and a telescoped crown (Alessandria Museum).

Grigio chiaro con bordo fuori grigio in tinta, cinta nera e cupola incavata in dentro (Museo di Alessandria).

1899

$\mathcal{A}$ gray felt hat with gray edging and a black band. A very elegant hat, for day use only. At night the top hat was still worn, and it remained the customary hat for all formal occasions (Alessandria Museum).

Feltro e bordo grigio, cinta nera. E' un cappello molto elegante, ma da giorno. Di sera si porta ancora il cilindro, che comunque resta il cappello da cerimonia di prammatica (Museo di Alessandria).

$\mathcal{A}$ light gray felt hat, with a raw edge and a narrow matching band. The brim could be shaped to one's taste (Alessandria Museum).

Feltro grigio chiaro sbordato, cinta bassa in tinta. L'ala può essere ripiegata a piacere (Museo di Alessandria).

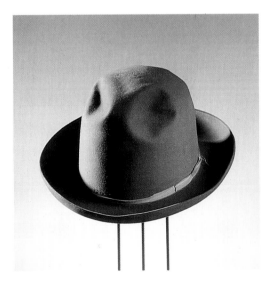

1 8 9 9

$\mathcal{A}$ light brown felt hat with matching band and edging on the outer side of the brim. It was intended to be worn while promenading down the main street of town, either on foot or in a carriage. On meeting a lady it was necessary to tip one's hat. In this way, at the dawn of the twentieth century, the hat was still being used to salute others and to win their good graces, just as it had been in the twelfth century (Alessandria Museum).

Feltro marroncino, bordo fuori e cinta in tinta. Adatto per la passeggiata sul corso, a piedi o in carrozza. Se si incontrano signore bisognerà "far di cappello". E così pure al nuovo secolo che sta per cominciare, per salutarlo e per acquistarsene la benevolenza, proprio com'era d'uso nel 1100 (Museo di Alessandria).

1 9 0 0

$\mathcal{A}$ shiny black silk-finish top hat with a flattened rolled-brim edge, a medium-tall crown, and a medium-wide band. The latter is silk, with a roll of ribbon to hide the seam where the loop is joined. The typical headgear of the middle and upper classes, this hat was worn both by snobbish social climbers in tails and court gentlemen of the old nobility (Monza Museum).

Cilindro nero lucido a pelo raso, bordo schiacciato, cupola e cinta medie, quest'ultima in seta e chiusa con cucitura a rollino. E' il copricapo delle classi medio-alte. Lo portano gli snob in marsina e lo portano i gentiluomini di corte di antica nobiltà (Museo di Monza).

A boater with a stiff brim and a wide band in two colors. This was the typical summer hat for all, regardless of class. It was worn by Oscar Wilde and Gabriele D'Annunzio, the philosopher Antonio Labriola, and Mussolini, together with a buttonhole flower and white gaiters. Almost up until 1940, this and the panama were the typical summer hats, to be worn beginning around May (Alessandria Museum).

Paglietta a tesa rigida con cinta alta bicolore. E' il tipico cappello estivo portato senza distinzione di classe. E' il copricapo che portava Oscar Wilde e che porta D'Annunzio; e anche Labriola; e anche Mussolini, fiore all'occhiello e ghette bianche. Fino quasi al 1940, accanto al panama è il cappello della bella stagione, detto "magiostrina" perché se ne iniziava l'uso verso maggio (Museo di Alessandria).

$\mathscr{A}$ gray, semi-hard hat with a high crown and a gray grosgrain outer-brim edging and band. This was one of the two fashionable models for daytime wear for this year (Alessandria Museum).

Cappello grigio semirigido a cupola alta, bordo fuori e cinta in canneté grigio. E' uno dei due modelli da giorno di moda quest'anno (Museo di Alessandria).

A gray hat with a raw edge and a cream-colored band. The brim could be turned up as desired; this was the other favorite model from 1901 (Alessandria Museum).

Cappello grigio sbordato con cinta crema. L'ala si rialza a piacere; è l'altro modello preferito del 1901 (Museo di Alessandria).

1 9 0 3

A red-brown felt hat with a raw edge and a wide band of the same color. Like the hat on the left, this one could take many shapes (Alessandria Museum).

Feltro marrone rossiccio sbordato, cinta alta in tinta. E' un cappello che, come il precedente, può assumere varie forme (Museo di Alessandria).

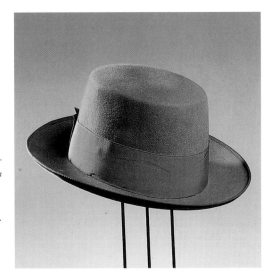

A burnt-brown felt hat with a raw edge and a band of three grosgrain ribbons in graduated shades from brown to beige. This could be a hat from the present day (Alessandria Museum).

Feltro sbordato in marrone bruciato con cinta formata da tre nastri di canneté, in gradazioni dal marrone al beige. Potrebbe essere un cappello dei nostri giorni (Museo di Alessandria).

*T*he year's fashion
offered three models that were
quite different in color and
shape. This is a tobacco-colored
felt hat with a sloping crown,
a matching band, and a brim
turned up at the sides
(Alessandria Museum).

La moda dell'anno suggerisce
tre modelli abbastanza dissimili
per colore e foggia. Questo è in
feltro color tabacco a cupola
inclinata, cinta in tinta e tese
rialzate lateralmente (Museo di
Alessandria).

$\mathcal{A}$ standard-crown felt hat, with a rather wide gray band and outer-brim edging (Alessandria Museum).

Feltro a cupola normale, cinta e bordo fuori grigi, piuttosto alti (Museo di Alessandria).

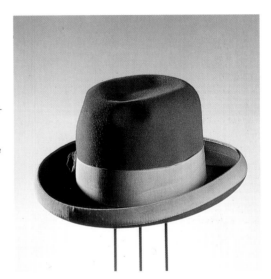

$\mathcal{A}$ black felt hat with black outer-brim edging and a black band ornamented with a large bow. The Wright Brothers' airplane was the latest craze. The brim (or "wing," in Italian) of this Borsalino was called the "eagle," and that of the first hat in this line was called the "kite." Everybody wanted to fly . . . (Alessandria Museum).

Feltro nero, bordo fuori nero, cinta nera abbellita da una gala importante. L'aeroplano dei fratelli Wright è recentissimo. L'ala di questo Borsalino si chiama "Aquila" e quella del primo di questo gruppo si chiama "Aquilone". Voglia di volare . . . (Museo di Alessandria).

$\mathscr{A}$ gray felt hat with a raw edge, a high crown, and a wide matching band, all very austere. A hat worthy of Giorgio Sonnino, an aristocratic and distinguished member of the Chamber of Deputies (Alessandria Museum).

Feltro grigio sbordato a cupola e cinta in tinta alte, molto austero. Degno di figurare in testa all'aristocratico onorevole Sonnino (Museo di Alessandria).

$\mathcal{A}$ greenish felt hat with a green band and outer-brim edging. As is typical of the unpredictable comings and goings of hat styles, this Borsalino is not very different from an 1899 model (Alessandria Museum).

Feltro verdino, cinta a bordo fuori verde. Come si addice agli strampalati corsi e ricorsi del cappello, questo Borsalino non è molto diverso dal quello del 1899 (Museo di Alessandria).

$\mathscr{A}$ blue felt hat with a band and outer-brim edging in matching silk gros-grain, a high crown, and a narrow brim. This model was intended to demonstrate the beauty, variety, and quality of the Italian hat, in order to reverse the London fashion of going bare-headed even in evening clothes, at balls, at the theater, in restaurants, and in carriages (Alessandria Museum).

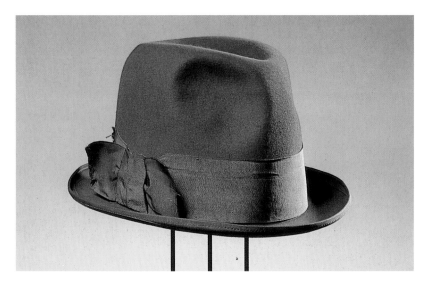

Feltro azzurro, bordo fuori e cinta in canneté di seta in tinta, cupola alta e ala stret-ta. Si tratta di un modello che mira a opporre bellezza, varietà e qualità del cappello italiano alla moda londinese di andare a testa nuda perfino in frac e smoking, al ballo, a teatro, al ristorante, in carrozza (Museo di Alessandria).

A matte gray top hat with a gray rolled brim edging and a black silk grosgrain band. As ever, elegance was considered the best revenge (Monza Museum).

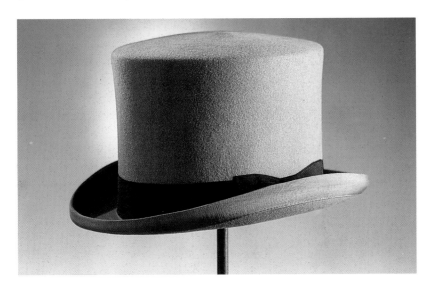

Cilindro grigio opaco, bordo grigio rollé, cinta in canneté di seta nera. Anche l'arma dell'eleganza è più che valida (Museo di Monza).

A classic top hat to be worn with formal clothes. The brilliantly shiny silk finish was meant to dazzle (Mutinelli Collection).

Cilindro classico da portare con l'abito da cerimonia. A pelo raso, lucidissimo: deve "sparare" (Collezione Mutinelli).

A black bowler with a rolled brim and a narrow ribbon band. This year's fashion was characterized by hard and semi-hard hats (Monza Museum).

Bombetta nera, ala rollé, cinta bassa a nastro. La moda dell'anno è caratterizzata dal cappello rigido e semirigido (Museo di Monza).

This dark gray felt Borsalino, with a raw edge and a paler-colored band, was called the "Doge." Venice had long ceased fighting the Turks, but Italy had fought them just this year and ended by conquering Libya (Alessandria Museum).

Questo modello Borsalino, in feltro grigio scuro, sbordato e con cinta in sottocolore, si chiama "Doge". Venezia ha cessato da molto di combattere contro i turchi. L'Italia, da pochissimo: e in conclusione ha conquistato la Libia (Museo di Alessandria).

$\mathscr{A}$ gray-green felt hat with matching outer-brim edging and a wide band with a bow in a deeper shade. In Italy, everything seemed peaceful, and fashion emphasized the elegance and security of the liberal-conservative classes (Alessandria Museum).

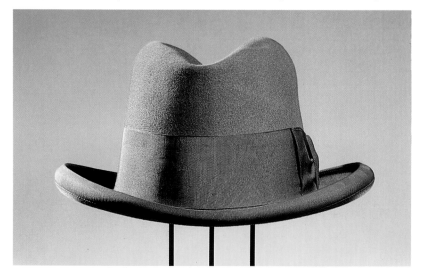

Feltro verde-grigio, cinta alta con gala arricciata in sopra colore, bordo fuori in tinta. In Italia tutto è ancora apparentemente tranquillo. La moda vuole sottolineare che si dà molto valore all'eleganza solida, sicura, dei rappresentanti della classe liberalcon-servatrice (Museo di Alessandria).

$\mathcal{T}$his Borsalino with a raw edge, a wide band, and a flat bow, was significantly named *Usbergo* ("Suit of Armor"). World War I had broken out, but Italy still maintained neutrality (Alessandria Museum).

Questo modello Borsalino sbordato con alta cinta a gala piatta si chiama, significativamente, "Usbergo". La guerra mondiale è scoppiata, ma l'Italia si mantiene ancora neutrale (Museo di Alessandria).

A dove-gray felt hat with a very high crown, a stitched inner-brim edging, and a grosgrain band in a deeper shade (Alessandria Museum).

Feltro color tortora a cupola molto alta, bordo dentro cucito, cinta in canneté sopracolore (Museo di Alessandria).

A gray felt hat with a crown that is almost a truncated cone, stitched edging inside the brim, and a wide matching band. Italy had gone to war, a move initiated by the Salandra government in order to conquer independent Italian-speaking territories. The style of this hat is somewhat reminiscent of the Risorgimento (Alessandria Museum).

Feltro a cupola quasi a tronco di cono, grigio scarso, bordo dentro cucito, cinta alta in tinta. L'Italia è entrata in guerra, una guerra inizialmente condotta dal governo Salandra per la conquista delle terre irredenti. Il cappello assume nuovamente un aspetto quasi risorgimentale (Museo di Alessandria).

$\mathcal{A}$ hat of rough mixed felt with a raw edge, a silk grosgrain band in a deeper shade, and a pleated bow, from Chiesa hatters (Mutinelli Collection). Now that peace had returned, all the Italian hat factories were competing madly to make hats suitable for both the new industrial class and those young men who lived solely for pleasure— or for power.

Feltro misto ruvido, sbordato, cinta in canneté di seta in sopracolore a gala arricciata della Cappelleria Chiesa (Collezione Mutinelli). Tutte le fabbriche di cappelli italiane fanno a gara, ora che è ritornato il sereno, nel produrre cappelli adatti sia alla nuova classe industriale, sia alla gioventù che punta solo al piacere o punta solo al potere.

A green-colored felt hat with a raw edge, a matching band, and a pinched crown (Monza Museum).

Feltro verdino, sbordato, cinta in tinta, bozze laterali (Museo di Monza).

$\mathcal{A}$ light gray felt hat with a matching gray outer-brim edging and a black band. This traditional hat is suitable for practically any occasion in elegant society (Monza Museum).

Feltro grigio chiaro, bordo fuori grigio in tinta, cinta nera. È un cappello che resta nel solco del tradizionale cappello per quasi ogni occasione della buona società (Museo di Monza).

$\mathcal{A}$ bowler with a black silk grosgrain outer-brim edging and a black band with a flat bow. This hat would remain in style for another twenty years or more. It was made popular by the Fascist party bosses, and also by Charlie Chaplin, who made the film *The Kid* in this year (Monza Museum).

Bombetta con bordo fuori e cinta a gala piatta in canneté di seta nera. Sarà di moda per il prossimo ventennio e oltre. A lanciarlo ci penseranno i gerarchi. E anche Charlie Chaplin, che quest'anno ha interpretato "Il monello" (Museo di Monza).

$\mathcal{A}$ very elegant gray felt hat with a matching band and outer-brim edging. The edging has three rows of stitching, and the band has a pleated bow. In the Borsalino line, this hat was the prototype for the "twenties style" (Alessandria Museum).

Elegantissimo feltro grigio con cinta e bordo fuori in tinta; il bordo presenta tre giri di piccature; la cinta, una gala arricciata. Nel campionario Borsalino figura come prototipo della "Moda 1920" (Museo di Alessandria).

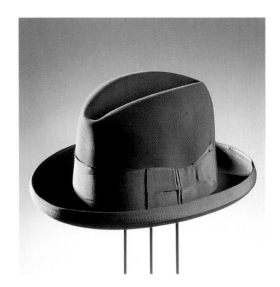

A silver-gray felt hat with a welt-edged brim with three rows of stitching and a black band (Mutinelli Collection). Two explosive developments had occurred in America: Rudolf Valentino and Prohibition, which made a good deal of money for gangsters smuggling whiskey by the truckload. In Milan, the explosion was real: an anarchist's bomb at the Diana music hall. Not everything was as pleasant as the style of this hat.

Feltro grigio argento ala ripiegata con tre serie di piccature cinta nera (Collezione Mutinelli). In America esplodono la bomba Rodolfo Valentino, i camion di whisky delle bande rivali (il proibizionismo fa fare soldi a palate); a Milano, una bomba al Diana. Non tutto è perbene come questo modello.

$\mathcal{T}$he typical sporting hat of the twenties: shorn black felt with a raw edge, a black band, and a wide brim (Mutinelli Collection). This was the kind of hat worn by Prime Minister Giolitti in Italy and by many gangster bosses in the States; in Lombardy, it was the hat that the ox merchants wore at fairs, along with a black cloak.

E' il tipico cappello sportivo degli Anni Venti: feltro nero rasato, sbordato, cinta nera, ala importante (Collezione Mutinelli). E' il cappello di Giolitti, il cappello di molti boss della mala negli States e, in Lombardia, perfino il cappello che i mercanti di buoi indossano alle fiere insieme con il tabarro, pure nero.

A dark gray felt hat with a wide band in a lighter shade and a brim with a welted edge and a row of stitching. A hat with a strangely old-fashioned look—possibly, in this turbulent year, a sign of nostalgic romanticism further encouraged by the success of the book *Addio, giovinezza*! ("*Farewell to Youth*") (Alessandria Museum).

Feltro grigio scuro, cinta alta in sottocolore, ala ripiegata in dentro con un giro di piccature. E' un cappello dall'aspetto stranamente vecchiotto; forse, in questo anno turbolento, un segno di romanticismo sollecitato anche dal successo della pubblicazione di "Addio, giovinezza!" (Museo di Alessandria).

*A*n ice-gray felt hat with a raw edge, a matching band, and a pinched crown. This hat could be shaped to one's taste (Alessandria Museum).

Feltro grigio ghiaccio, sbordato, cinta in tinta, bozze laterali. Si può sagomare a piacere (Museo di Alessandria).

A soft hat in a beautiful shade of blue, with a raw edge and a band that is almost violet. The brim could be shaped as desired (Monza Museum).

Cappello floscio di un bellissimo tono di blu, sbordato, cinta quasi viola, ala sagomabile a piacere (Museo di Monza).

A dark gray felt hat. With its Fascist black band and German-style edging, this was the hat of ultimate respectablity for the times. Although Mussolini had denounced the Aventino political group as seditious, in private he wore hats like this one, or his beloved bowler (Alessandria Museum).

Feltro grigio scuro, bordatura "tedesca" in fuori. Ancora una variante del cappello bene per eccellenza. Soprattutto per il colore della cinta (nero) e per il nome della bordatura: dati i tempi . . . Mussolini denuncia l'Aventino come organizzazione sediziosa; in privato, indossa cappelli come questo o l'amata bombetta (Museo di Alessandria).

$\mathscr{A}$ greenish felt hat with a gray-green outer-brim edging and a wide reddish band. Paris was wild about the Charleston, but the anti-Fascist leader Pietro Nenni, shown wearing a similar hat in a rare photograph, was now an exile in France and had other things on his mind (Alessandria Museum).

*Feltro verdino, bordo fuori
grigio-verde, cinta alta rossiccia.
A Parigi impazza il charleston;
Pietro Nenni, ritratto con un
cappello simile in una rara foto,
esule in Francia ha altro a cui
pensare (Museo di Alessandria).*

1928

$\mathcal{A}$ mouse-gray felt hat with a raw edge, a wide band of blue-black grosgrain, and a pinched crown. This model lent itself to many different occasions and shapings. It could be worn with the brim turned down in the center, or turned up on one side and down on the other, as was the fashion for Mussolini and his cronies during their early-morning horseback rides in the park at the Villa Borghese (Alessandria Museum).

Feltro grigio topo, sbordato, cinta alta in canneté blu-nero bozze laterali. E' un modello che si presta a più occasioni e fogge. Può essere portato con l'ala reclinata verso il basso al centro o sollevata da una parte e reclinata dall'altra, come usano fare Mussolini e fedelissimi di mattina presto, al galoppo a Villa Borghese (Museo di Alessandria).

*A*n orange felt hat with an unbordered brim with all-over stitching and a pinched crown with a square pattern of dark stripes and yellow stitching. The hatband is made of two different bicolored cords, knotted at the side. This very modern hat was made in Monza for the African market (Monza Museum).

Feltro arancione con ala sbordata e piccata, cupola a bozze a righe scure e piccature gialle che formano un disegno a quadri. Cinta formata da due diversi cordoncini bicolori annodati lateralmente. E' un cappello prodotto a Monza per il mercato africano, singolarmente moderno (Museo di Monza).

A superb "diplomatic" hat of dove-gray shorn felt with a matching silk grosgrain outer-brim edging and band (Mutinelli Collection). This hat is almost a symbol of the thirties, a decade of great movements led by great men with grand, secret goals and grand, rosy hopes.

Un magnifico cappello "diplomatico" in feltro rasato color tortora con bordo fuori e cinta in canneté di seta in tinta (Collezione Mutinelli). Quasi un simbolo di questo decennio di grandi andirivieni, nel mondo, di grandi personaggi con grandi, segrete mire e grandi, rosee speranze.

1 9 3 0

$\mathcal{L}$ess luxurious, in fact a type that could be called subdued, is this felt hat in classic gray, with a thin matching outer-brim edging and a wide black band (Alessandria Museum).

Meno di gran lusso, di un genere per cosi dire sommesso, questo feltro in classico grigio, bordo fuori sottile in tinta e alta cinta nera (Museo di Alessandria).

1 9 3 5

$\mathcal{A}$ black bowler with a black silk grosgrain outer-brim edging and band. This was the favorite headgear of Mussolini, who had a wide range of derbies in every color. He went without them only when he had to go into the country to publicize his famous "battle of the grain" (Alessandria Museum).

Bombetta nera con bordo fuori e cinta in canneté di seta nera. E' il copricapo preferito di Mussolini che possiede un vero repertorio di bombette di ogni colore. Se ne priva giusto se deve andare in campagna a promuovere la famosa "banaglia del grano" (Museo di Alessandria).

Another bowler, with a black grosgrain inner-brim edging and band. This was the typical headgear for men who wore a stiff wing collar, a black tie, and a waistcoat (Alessandria Museum).

Un'altra bombetta, bordo in dentro e cinta in canneté nero. E' il copricapo tipico dell'uomo che porta il colletto duro a punte triangolari, cravatta nera e gilet (Museo di Alessandria).

1 9 3 7

$\mathscr{A}$ derby with a false-trimmed edge and a black band. Fashion continued to be inspired by the great historical figures of the moment. The same attire, however—bowler, stiff collar, and waist-coat—was also worn by Charlie Chaplin this year, as the hero of the film *Modern Times* (Alessandria Museum).

Bombetta con bordo finto e cinta nera. La moda che si ispira ai grandi personaggi del momento continua. Solo che questo stesso abbigliamento: bombetta, colletto duro e gilet, lo porta anche Charlot, protagonista, quest'anno, di "Tempi Moderni" (Museo di Alessandria).

1 9 4 2

$\mathscr{A}$ gray felt hat with a matching outer-brim edging and a wide black band. In a famous poster, Winston Churchill wore a hat just like this one. Hats changed very little during this time. Italy had just entered the war, which was raging across the continent, and almost every man in Europe was at the front, wearing military headgear (Alessandria Museum).

Feltro grigio, bordo fuori in tinta e cinta alta nera. La guerra è scoppiata nel 1940. Da un manifesto divenuto famoso Winston Churchill è ritratto con un cappello perfettamente identico a questo. I cappelli non presentano variazioni apprezzabili. Quasi tutti gli uomini europei sono al fronte e portano copricapi militari (Museo di Alessandria).

A steel-gray, beaver-finished felt hat with a raw edge and a chained felt band (Mutinelli Collection). Europe was at peace again, and hat shops had a good selection of new models, better suited to hopes for a bright future.

Feltro grigio acciaio, sbordato, lavorazione flamand (pelo lungo), cinta in feltro listellato (Collezione Mutinelli). La pace è conclusa. Nelle cappellerie fanno bella mostra di sé nuovi modelli, più adatti alle speranze di un ormai possibile futuro radioso.

1 9 4 5

$\mathscr{A}$ silver-gray beaver-finished felt with a raw edge, a narrow matching felt band, and a pinched crown (right)(Mutinelli Collection).

Feltro grigio argento, lavorazione flamand, sbordato, cinta bassa di feltro in tinta, bozze laterali (a destra)(Collezione Mutinelli).

1 9 4 6

$\mathscr{A}$ sporty lead-gray felt hat with a self-trimmed edge and a matching mat-work wool band (right, below)(Monza Museum).

Feltro grigio piombo sportivo, bordo finto, cinta di lana lavorata a stuoia in tinta (a destra, sotto)(Museo di Monza).

1 9 4 5

$\mathscr{A}$ short top hat of sea-blue shorn felt, with a turned-up brim and a white silk outer-brim edging and band (below)(Mutinelli Collection).

Mezzo cilindro in feltro rasato blu marin, ala ripiegata, bordo fuori e cinta in seta bianca (sotto)(Collezione Mutinelli).

A light beige felt hat with a raw edge and the rather wide brim that was typical of this type of hat during the forties. The elegant brown silk band has a flat bow (Monza Museum).

Feltro beige chiaro, sbordato, ala piuttosto larga tipica del decennio per questo tipo di cappello, elegante cinta in seta marrone a gala piatta (Museo di Monza).

$\mathscr{A}$ gray felt hat with a matching outer-brim edging and a wide black band. This was still the classic model for important occasions (Alessandria Museum).

Feltro grigio, bordo fuori in tinta, cinta alta nera. Per le occasioni più importanti, questo modello è il classico di sempre (Museo di Alessandria).

A rare and prized undyed natural nutria-fur hat, made to measure for Teresio Usuelli, Giuseppe Borsalino's great-grandson, who later became the president of the company. The hat has a raw edge and is decorated with a row of paired holes halfway up the crown. A nutria hat can be folded, rolled up, and generally abused because it always springs back into shape (Usuelli Borsalino Collection).

Un raro e pregiato cappello di pelo di nutria naturale, non tinto, fatto su misura per il Signor Teresio Usuelli, pronipote di Giuseppe Borsalino e divenuto poi presidente della Società. Il cappello è sbordato, a mezza cupola decorata con un serie di forellini a coppia. Il cappello di nutria può essere ripiegato, arrotolato, maltratta- to: ritorna sempre in forma (Collezione Usuelli Borsalino).

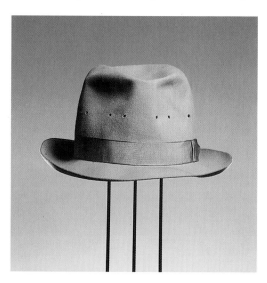

*A*n ice-gray felt hat with a raw edge and a dark silk grosgrain band. This model was designed for the winter season (Alessandria Museum).

Feltro sbordato, color ghiaccio con cinta in canneté di seta scura. E' un modello studiato per la stagione invernale (Museo di Alessandria).

A gray-green felt hat with a stitched edge and a brown band with a pleated bow. Hats were still widely worn during the years immediately after the war, partly because indoor heating was not the best, and partly because men felt a need to dress like civilians from head to toe. And they were free to do so: the Italian republic was now a reality (Alessandria Museum).

Feltro grigio-verde, bordo piccato, cinta marrone con gala arricciata. E' ancora il primo dopoguerra e il cappello è molto portato, un po' perché il riscaldamento non è ottimale, un po' perché gli uomini sentono il bisogno di vestirsi in borghese dalla testa ai piedi. Liberamente: in Italia, è l'anno della Costituzione della Repubblica (Museo di Alessandria).

A gray felt hat with a raw edge and a gray-beige band; holes are punched in a star shape on the side of the crown, with the same motif centered on the crown. Along with phonograph records, American films from the forties had made a belated debut in Italy, influencing styles somewhat (Alessandria Museum).

Feltro grigio sbordato, cinta grigio-beige; sulla cupola, un traforo a stella laterale e un identico motivo traforato centrale. Come i dischi, anche i film americani Anni Quaranta arrivano in ritardo. E un po' la moda vi si ispira (Museo di Alessandria).

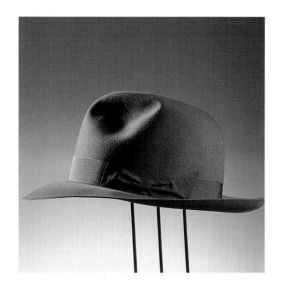

𝒜 gray felt hat with an edge and a black band with a flat bow with flared ends. The brim could be folded in various ways so that the hat could be reshaped to suit the occasion (Alessandria Museum).

Feltro grigio sbordato, cinta nera con gala piatta a punte sporgenti. L'ala si può ripiegare in vari modi e il cappello può quindi variare di forma adattandosi alle circostanze (Museo di Alessandria).

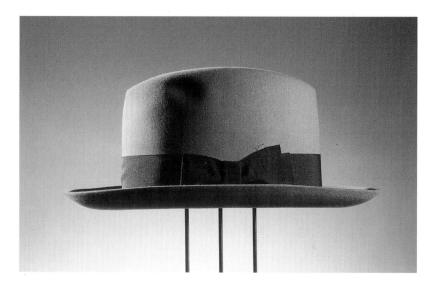

A blue felt hat with matching outer-brim edging and band. It was worn as shown, but only with an elegant outfit, such as a gray or blue suit with a camel-hair coat (Alessandria Museum).

Feltro blu, bordo fuori e cinta in tinta. Si porta così, ma del resto è destinato solo ad un abbigliamento elegante, per esempio abito grigio o blu e cappotto di pelo di cammello (Museo di Alessandria).

*A*n extra-light shorn felt hat, or foulard, in light beige, with a brown silk grosgrain band with a flat bow. It weighs only two ounces (Mutinelli Collection). This hat could be seen as a way of celebrating the first fifty years of the century, expressing this wish: May the second half of the century be easy and light, floating toward the year 2000 like a feather!

Feltro rasato superpiuma (o foulard) beige tenue, cinta marrone in canneté di seta a gala piatta. Pesa solo gr 60 (Collezione Mutinelli). Per festeggiare le nozze d'argento del secolo XX, quasi un augurio: che l'altra metà sia lieve, che voli leggera verso il 2000 come una piuma!

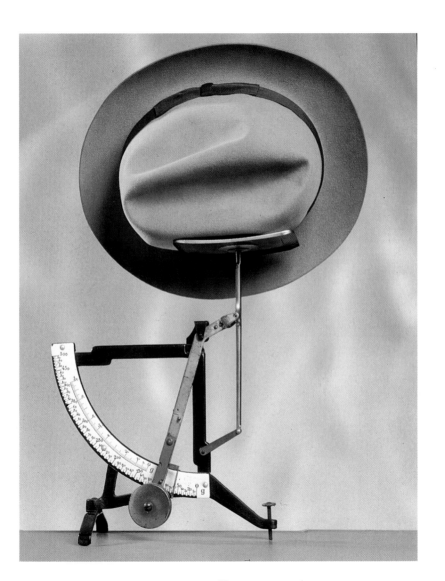

A classic gray felt hat for the second half of the century, with felted edging and a band in a deeper shade (Alessandria Museum).

Il classico feltro grigio in versione seconda metà del secolo: bordo feltrato, cinta in sopracolore (Museo di Alessandria). ➢

A sporty felt hat in light gray with a narrow brim edging, a narrow ribbon band knotted at the side, and a tele-scoped crown. It goes well with a duffle coat (Alessandria Museum).

Feltro sportivo, grigio chiaro, bordo sottile, cinta a nastrino annodata lateralmente, cupola schiacciata. Va bene anche col Montgomery (Museo di Alessandria).

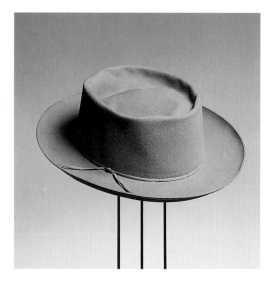

A double-stitched oat-colored straw hat, with a silk foulard hatband with yellow polka dots and a telescoped crown. Italians were beginning to vacation at the beach again, and Capri was "in" (Alessandria Museum).

Paglia d'avena cucita doppia, cinta in foulard di seta a pois gialli, cupola schiacciata. Si riprende ad andare in vacanza al mare. Capri è di gran moda (Museo di Alessandria).

A gray-green felt hat with a stitched edge, a crown with side welting, and a felt band with a chained pattern on the sides. For winter vacations in the mountains, where people drive in their sporty new Fiats and Lancias (Alessandria Museum).

Feltro verde-grigio, bordo piccato, cupola con nervature laterali, cinta in feltro listellato lateralmente. Per le vacanze d'inverno, in montagna, dove si va con le nuove auto sportive Fiat e Lancia (Museo di Alessandria).

A dark gray felt hat with a matching silk grosgrain outer-brim edging and band. A very elegant hat, suitable for accompanying mink-wrapped ladies through the showrooms of couturiers in Rome and Milan, or Paris, still the undisputed capital of fashion (Alessandria Museum).

Feltro grigio scuro, bordo fuori e cinta di canneté di seta in tinta. Di grande eleganza, adatto per accompagnare le signore in visone negli ateliers di Roma e Milano. O di Parigi, ancora incontrastata capitale della moda (Museo di Alessandria).

 $\mathcal{A}$ black bowler with a false-trimmed edge and a *dorsé* rolled brim. For Englishmen who preferred Italian brands, or for Italians going to England to reopen the international market (Alessandria Museum).

Bombetta nera, bordo finto, ala dorsé rolé. Per gli inglesi che preferiscono le marche italiane o per gli italiani che si recano in Inghilterra per riaprire il mercato internazionale (Museo di Alessandria).

 $\mathcal{A}$ shiny, silk-finished, fur-felt top hat, with a self-trimmed edge and a silk grosgrain band with a flat bow. In the near future, this kind of hat would be worn to La Scala by operagoers eager to witness the triumphs of the divine Maria Callas (Alessandria Museum).

Cilindro a pelo raso, lucido, bordo finto, cinta in canneté di seta a gala piatta. Tra poco lo si porterà per andare ad assistere, alla Scala, ai trionfi della divina Maria Callas (Museo di Alessandria).

Traditional Hats

$\mathcal{I}$talian production for the foreign market has always been noteworthy for both its quality and its quantity. As early as 1900, Borsalino was already exporting three hats abroad for every two sold in Italy. Giuseppe Borsalino himself, leaving for a mountain-climbing excursion in Australia at age seventy, did not forget to take his sample case along. He returned after having conquered the Australian market. The factories of Monza also exported all over the world. Here are some examples of hats made for the foreign market, not counting some of the bowlers shown on preceding pages.

Cappelli Tipici

La produzione per l'estero è sempre stata notevole sia qualitativamente che quantitativamente. La Borsalino, già nel 1900, su due cappelli per l'Italia ne produceva tre per l'estero. Lo stesso Giuseppe Borsalino, partito a sessant'anni per l'Australia per fare alpinismo, non dimenticò di portare con sé il campionario. Ritornò dopo essersi conquistato il mercato australiano. Anche le fabbriche monzesi esportavano in tutto il mondo. Ed ecco alcuni esempi di produzione per l'estero, esclusa la bombetta già più volte illustrata.

Austria and Tyrol

$\mathcal{A}$ black felt hat with a raw edge. The high crown is almost entirely covered by a green silk grosgrain band, ornamented with black braid around the middle and a rooster feather at the back (Monza Museum).

Austria e Tirolo

Feltro nero sbordato a cupola alta quasi interamente ricoperta di canneté di seta verde ornato al centro da un gallone nero; piume di gallo sulla parte posteriore (Museo di Monza).

Austria and Tyrol

Austria and Tyrol

A roundish black felt hat, with an outer-brim edging of red fabric, a low crown, and a red fabric band ornamented with gold braid and a red feather (Monza Museum).

Austria e Tirolo

Feltro nero tondeggiante, bordo fuori in panno rosso, cupola bassa, cinta in panno rosso ornata da un gallone dorato e una penna rossa (Museo di Monza).

Spain

A 1920 cream-colored "Sevillano," with a matching narrow outer-brim edging, a stiff brim, a silk band in a deeper shade, and a flat bow with flared ends (Monza Museum).

Spagna

Cappello "sivigliano" color crema, piccolo bordo fuori in tinta, ala rigida, cinta in seta a gala piatta con punte sporgenti in seta sopracolore, 1920 (Museo di Monza).

Spain

A black "Sevillano," with a low, flat crown, a stiff brim, a black silk grosgrain band with a flat bow, and a red silk lining (Alessandria Museum).

Spagna
"Sivigliano" nero a cupola bassa e piatta, ala rigida, cinta nera in canneté di seta a gala piatta, fodera in seta rossa (Museo di Alessandria).

$\mathcal{A}$ small *calañés*, an Andalusian cap of brick-red velvet with a tilted, slightly conical crown and high, deeply curled-in brim (Alessandria Museum).

Spagna

Piccolo calañés, cappello andaluso in velluto rosso mattone, cupola leggermente conica reclinata, tese molto rialzate in dentro (Museo di Alessandria).

African Countries

These hats are typical not of folk tradition but of a certain kind of noncon-
formist taste that survived up until the twenties and thirties.

Paesi africani

*Non tipici quanto a tipo di cappello, ma quanto a un certo tipo di gusto molto anticon-
formista, almeno fino agli anni '20-'30.*

At right: a velvet hat in a tiger print, from 1930 (Monza Museum). Right,
below: A black felt hat with the edge and brim lined with yellow canvas, and a yellow
band in a tiger print. It was probably intended for South Africa, as is suggested by the
brim's being buttoned on only one side. From the 1920s (Monza Museum). Below: A
South African hat with a raw edge, a wide brim, a narrow matching band knotted on the
side with a tuft of feathers, and a high, pinched crown (Alessandria Museum).

*A destra, sopra: Cappello in
velluto stampato a motivo
"tigre", 1930 (Museo di
Monza). A destra, sotto:
Cappello in feltro nero, bordo e
ala foderati in tela gialla, cinta
gialla stampata a motivo
"tigre". Verosimilmente destinato al Sudafrica come indica
l'ala abbottonata lateralmente
da una sola parte. Anni '20
(Museo di Monza). A destra:
Cappello sudafricano sbordato,
a tesa larga, cinta bassa in
tinta annodata lateralmente
insieme con un ciuffetto di
piume, cupola alta a bozze
(Museo di Alessandria).*

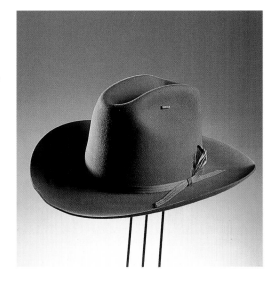

Pith Helmets

These helmet-type sun hats were habitually worn mainly by residents of Africa and India during the colonial era.

Coloniali

Cappelli a casco abitualmente portati soprattutto dai residenti in Africa e in India in età coloniale.

The "rosette" on the inside of the hat, which allowed ventilation (Alessandria Museum).

La "rosetta" che serve a far circolare l'aria (Museo di Alessandria).

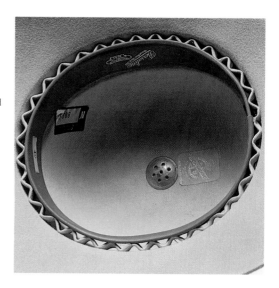

$\mathscr{A}$ gray felt helmet with a stiff brim, and a stepped crown with a rosette at the top (Alessandria Museum).

Coloniale in feltro grigio, ala rigida, cupola sagomata con "rosetta" in cima (Museo di Alessandria).

A gray felt helmet with outer-brim edging, a draped silk band with a gray-on-gray stripe, and a rosette at the top of the crown. It is very similar to a standard stiff hat (Alessandria Museum).

Coloniale in feltro grigio, bordo fuori, cinta drappeggiata in seta a righe grigio su grigio, "rosetta" al centro cupola. E' molto simile a un normale cappello duro (Museo di Alessandria).

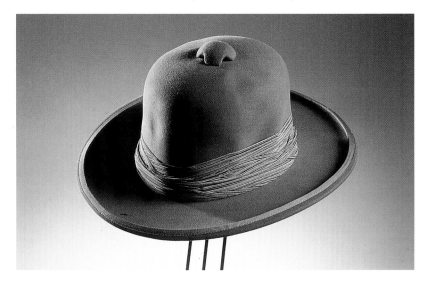

$\mathcal{A}$ dark beige helmet with a wide, pleated silk band and a tall crown with a rosette; from 1920 (Monza Museum).

Coloniale beige scuro, cinta alta in seta pieghettata, cupola alta con rosetta, 1920 (Museo di Monza).

$\mathcal{A}$ helmet with a stepped crown and a rosette, with brim edging and a band in a paler shade; from 1920 (Monza Museum).

Coloniale a cupola sagomata, con "rosetta", ala bordata e cinta in sottocolore, 1920 (Museo di Monza).

$\mathscr{A}$ *terai* (a large hunting helmet) of beige felt, with outer- and inner-brim edging of red fabric, a beige and red cotton muslin band, and a red felt rosette; from about 1906 (Alessandria Museum).

Teray (casco da caccia grossa) in feltro beige, bordo fuori e interno dell'ala in tessuto rosso, cinta in mussolina di cotone beige e rosso, "rosetta" in feltro rosso, ca 1906 (Museo di Alessandria).

The Fez, or Tarboosh

A stiff hat, usually in the form of a truncated cone, worn by Arabs, Turks (up to 1925), and Indian Muslims. It may or may not have a tassel.

Fez, o Tarbush

Copricapo di solito a cono tronco, rigido, portato da arabi, turchi (fino al 1925) e musulmani indiani. Può o no avere un fiocco.

Below, left: A white wool felt fez decorated with a centered tufts; from 1930. Below, right: An aubergine-colored Indian fez with a velvet band in a deeper shade at the base. Krizia made this the signature hat for the showing of her Indian-inspired 1985–86 winter collection. Right: A very tall, tubular red fez decorated with a short black tassel; from 1920 (Monza Museum).

Sotto, a sinistra: Fez di feltro di lana bianco decorato al centro da un pippiolino, 1930. Sotto, a destra: Fez indiano color aubergine con nastro di velluto sopracolore alla base. Krizia ne ha fatto il copricapo-simbolo della sfilata della sua collezione invernale 1985/86 ispirata all'India. A destra: Fez rosso, molto alto e a tubo, decorato da un corto fiocco nero, 1920 (Museo di Monza).

China

A black silk toque with two sets of
padded pleats, with a pompon and lining of red silk
(Alessandria Museum).

Cina
*Tocco in seta nera con due serie di piegoline imbot-
tite, pompon e fodera in seta rossa (Museo di
Alessandria).*

Japan

These are not traditional Japanese hats, but rather hats made in Monza for Japanese import, in shapes and colors to coordinate with the traditional men's costume, which was still very widely worn until just before the war.

Giappone

Non si tratta di cappelli tipici, quanto di cappelli che la produzione monzese destinava specificamente a questo paese adattandone foggia e colori agli abiti maschili nazionali, ancora molto portati fino a prima della guerra.

A beige felt hat printed with green maple leaves, with a silk cord band tied at the side; from about 1930 (Monza Museum).

Feltro beige stampato a foglie di acero verdi, cinta in cordoncino di seta annodata di lato, ca 1930 (Museo di Monza).

Japan

A rosy beige felt hat printed with a darker pattern of a stylized little motif, a raw edge, and a brown velvet band with a flat bow; from about 1930 (Monza Museum).

Giappone

Feltro beige rosato stampato a piccoli motivi stilizzati più scuri, sbordato, cinta in velluto marrone a gala piatta, ca 1930 (Museo di Monza).

United States

A cowboy hat with a typical high crown decorated on the sides with leather in a deeper shade, a band of the same leather, and a turned-up brim; from 1920 (Monza Museum).

Stati Uniti

"Cow-boy" con tipica cupola alta decorata di lato in pelle sopracolore, cinta a nastro della stessa pelle, ala rialzata, 1920 (Museo di Monza).

United States

$\mathscr{A}$ Texan hat of dark dove-gray felt, with a light gray grosgrain outer-brim edging and band; from 1947 (Alessandria Museum).

Stati Uniti
Cappello texano in feltro tortora scuro, bordo fuori e cinta in canneté grigio chiaro, 1947 (Museo di Alessandria).

South America

$\mathcal{A}$ hat made by Borsalino for Brazil: light dove-gray felt, with outer-brim edging and a ribbon band tied in a bow with raised loops; from 1950 (Alessandria Museum).

Stati Uniti

Cappello prodotto dalla Borsalino per il Brasile; feltro tortora chiaro, bordo fuori e cinta in tinta annodata a nastro con punte rialzate, 1950 (Museo di Alessandria).

Central America

A ceremonial Mexican *charro*, embroidered with narrow braid under the brim and ornamented with several windings of a tasseled silk cord around the crown; from 1915 (Monza Museum).

America Centrale
Charro messicano da cerimonia, ricamato a cordoncino sotto la tesa e ornato intorno alla cupola da più giri di cordone di seta terminante a nappa, 1915 (Museo di Monza).

A Bolivian *chola* of brown felt, with outer-brim edging and band of paler-colored silk. The band and bow are decorated with a velvet cord ending in pompons, and the bow has a little mother-of-pearl buckle (Alessandria Museum).

America del Sud

Chola boliviano in feltro marrone bordo fuori e cinta in seta sottocolore; cinta e gala sono decorate con cordoncino di velluto terminante a pompons e da una piccola fibbia di madreperla (Museo di Alessandria).

A gray felt hat, with a raw edge, a wide brim, and a black band, made by Borsalino for Colombia (Alessandria Museum).

America del Sud
Cappello in feltro grigio sbordato, ala larga, cinta nera, prodotto dalla Borsalino per la Columbia (Museo di Alessandria).

Hats and Hatmakers

These are the beginnings of the wool felt hats typical of the Monza factories: a little pile of wool ready for felting; a large felt cone made by steaming a disk cut from the felt; and a smaller cone obtained by shrinking the larger cone onto the appropriate mold. Felting was once done mechanically by steaming with harmful chemical additives, including mercuric nitrate. It was perhaps because of this that hatters were famous for being a bit mad (Monza Museum).

Capelli & Capella:

Così nasce il cappello di feltro di lana, tipico delle fabbriche di Monza: un mucchietto di lana già pronta per la feltratura; un grande feltro di forma conica ottenuto sotto ponendo a vaporizzazione un disco ritagliato nel feltro; un cono più piccolo ottenuto incapsulando il primo su apposite forme. A sua volta la feltratura era stata ottenuta meccanicamente e mediante umidificazione con coadiuvanti chimici nocivi tra cui il nitrato acido di mercurio. Forse per questo i cappellai hanno fama di essere un po' matti (Museo di Monza).

Hats can be mad, too. This is the typical headgear worn by the workers at Borsalino. They made these hats themselves, always in the same shape: a handmade skullcap, usually gray but sometimes green (Usuelli Borsalino Collection).

Anche il cappello può essere matto. Questo è il tipico copricapo che portavano gli operai della Borsalino. Lo facevano da sé, sempre di questa forma: uno zucchetto fatto a mano, di solito grigio e qualche volta verde (Collezione Usuelli Borsalino).

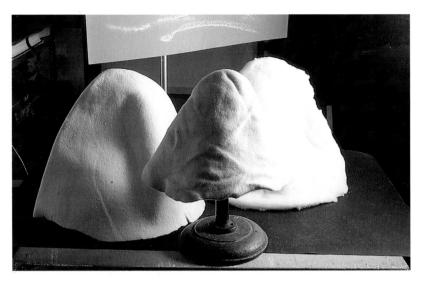

111

On the occasion of the company's centenary (1957), the hatmakers made this hat by hand for Signora Giovanna Usuelli Borsalino. Its crown and very broad brim (about 2 feet wide) are a single, seamless piece of rabbit-fur felt (Usuelli Borsalino Collection).

Per la signora Giovanna Usuelli Borsalino, in occasione del centenario dell'azienda (1957) i cappellai ne fecero uno a mano, con cupola e ala larghissima (c.a. 60 cm) in un solo pezzo, senza cucitura, in feltro di coniglio (Collezione Usuelli Borsalino).

*U*ntil the early days of our century, hat shops not only sold hats but made them as well, from felt hoods bought from the factory. This is the Mutinelli hat shop, founded in Milan one hundred years ago, just outside the local trade-tariff zone, at the end of the elegant Corso di Porta Orientale, an area known today as Porta Venezia (Mutinelli Collection).

Fino ai primi del nostro secolo, le cappellerie non solo vendevano, ma anche confezionavano cappelli, comprando dalle fabbriche i coni di feltro. Questa è la Cappelleria Mutinelli, fondata a Milano proprio 100 anni fa, appena fuori dazio dove terminava l'elegante Corso di Porta Orientale, oggi Porta Venezia (Collezione Mutinelli).

*W*earing top hats, dignitaries escort King Vittorio Emanuele III at the International Exposition of Industry in Milan in 1916 (Mutinelli Collection).

Portano la tuba i dignitari che scortano a Milano il Re Vittorio Emanuele III in visita all'Esposizione Internazionale del Lavoro del 1916 (Collezione Mutinelli).

*P*assing through the gates at Porta Orientale in a carriage or horse-drawn tram, people arrived at what is now Piazzale Loreto to attend a popular show given by the famous Milanese singer and storyteller Enrico Mulacchio, known as "il Barbapedana." He wore a short top hat, like the ones worn by chimney sweeps and coachmen (Mutinelli Collection).

Passati i cancelli di Porta Orientale si arrivava, in carrozza o col tram a cavalli, dove ora si trova Piazzale Loreto, per assistere allo spettacolo del celebre cantastorie meneghino Enrico Mulacchio detto il Barbapedana. Che in testa portava una mezza tuba. A Milano la portavano anche gli spazza-camini e i brumisti (Collezione Mutinelli).

Il famoso "Barba pedana" Enrico Malacchio -

Torrani

MILANO
VIA VERZIERE 18

$\mathcal{F}$or made-to-order stiff hats and boaters, the stores used this bizarre apparatus, which looks almost like an emperor's crown as painted by Enrico Baj. It was called "the informer." This is a French version from 1920 (Mutinelli Collection).

Nei negozi, per i cappelli duri e le pagliette su misura, si usava un buffo attrezzo che sembra quasi una corona da imperatore del Baj: l'informatore. Questo, francese, è del 1920 (Collezione Mutinelli).

$\mathcal{T}$he device has two parts, the "conformer" and the "informer." The rods are spread apart around the client's head to supply "information" about the "conformation" of his cranium. The gauge sticks then translate the results into centimeters (Monza Museum).

L'attrezzo ha due parti, conformatore e informatore: allargandosi, le bacchette aderivano alla testa del cliente per poter "informare" sulla "conformazione" del cranio. Le aste ne davano poi la traduzione in centimetri (Museo di Monza).

Another piece of shop equipment: the hat stretcher. Not that the head normally increases in volume; sometimes the wrong hat size is bought by mistake, or often a hat is handed down or traded among relatives, employees, and friends. This wooden piece dates from 1910 (Mutinelli Collection).

Altro attrezzo da negozio: l'allargacappelli. Non che normalmente la testa aumenti di volume ma, acquisti sbagliati a parte, il cappello è famoso per la sua riciclabilità a parenti, dipendenti ecc. Questo, in legno, è del 1910 (Collezione Mutinelli). ➤

A bit less outlandish, this measuring device for in-store use dates from 1920 to 1930. Made of sprung steel sheeting, it was slipped inside a hat to measure its circumference. In short, it was a more modern "informer" that measured the hat instead of the head (Mutinelli Collection).

Di aspetto meno stravagante, questo misuratore da negozio del 1920-30 è in lamina d'acciaio a molla. Posto all'interno del cappello ne misura la circonferenza. E' insomma un informatore più moderno ma ... per procura (Collezione Mutinelli).

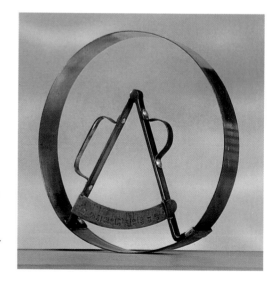

*I*n the days before time-saving, anonymous paper or plastic bags had been invented, the client left the shop with a smart hatbox. The box at right, modeled by a top hat, probably originally came with a dainty ladies' hat.

Quando ancora non usavano i sacchetti, cialtroni, di carta anonma o di plastica, il cliente usciva dal negozio con un elegante contenitore per cappelli. Il contenitore per cappelli a destra, modellato da un cilindro, probabilmente veniva originalmente con un delicato cappello da donna.

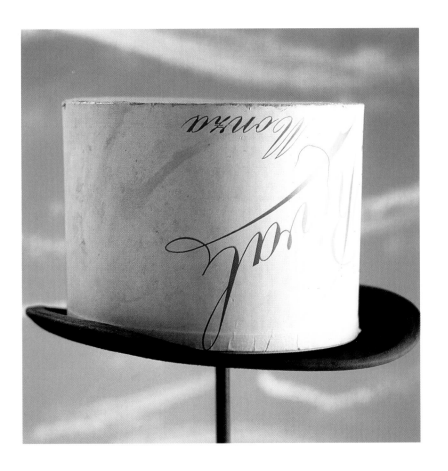

Men's Hats

Adolf Loos, an Austrian who was eccentric in more than one respect, was by profession an architect, though his father was a simple craftsman. It's difficult to express the full reach of Loos's independence of mind, judgment, and invention, but it may be useful to repeat here one of this architect's many typically caustic sayings: "Everybody knows I do not include architects in the category of human beings."

Why bring up Loos when the subject is hats? Above all, because while he frequently favored revolutionary solutions, Loos always maintained a profound bond not only with the great tradition of architecture, but also with that of craftsmanship. He wrote: "If nothing more than a button remained of a vanished civilization, from the shape of that button one might work one's way back up to that civilization's clothing and habits, its religion and customs, its art and spiritual life. Such indeed is the importance of a little button, and by emphasizing this I mean to say that there is a link between external and internal civilization: God creates the artist, the artist creates the age, the age creates the craftsman—and the craftsman creates the button."

Loos's words seem even truer when we contemplate apparently inert and lifeless objects that not only enhance and enliven our life, but also seem to be an expression of it. It was not by accident that Loos—an independent thinker who stood apart from the overwhelming movement of the Sezession, Austria's version of Art Nouveau—wrote about men's hats. Out of all the objects in our everyday life, a man's hat might be called the most independent in the absolute sense, answering only to its own inner laws. Unlike women's hats and even other forms of men's headgear, men's hats have not been greatly influenced by ephemeral fashion, which is always intent on "changing and rising again in more graceful forms," according to Giuseppe Parini, who dedicated the first part of his poem "Il Giorno" ("Day") to this "exquisitely charming goddess." In its own way, the hat (or its absence) has always defined specific cultures. The hat reveals, in fact, what is inside the head.

For example, there are cultures of the cap, of the turban, of the Macedonian *kausia*; of diadems of precious gems or precious eagle feathers, of the hood, and of the bare head. And then there are cultures of the hat.

CHANGES IN HAT STYLES

Throughout its long history, the man's hat has never lost its profound, total, and unpredictable freedom from definition. The top hat, for example, was worn by subversives, revolutionaries, and executioners, but later it became an indispensable part of the dandy's wardrobe, and of the formal uniform of English army officers. Hat preferences don't follow any rationale, so that we see the same type of top hat worn by the diabolical cartoon character Mandrake the Magician and by a pious personage drawn by Dürer in the prayer book of Emperor Maximilian I. Tiny Toulouse-Lautrec wore a towering stovepipe, while the sophisticated Robert de Montesquiou-Fezensac wore one of harmonious proportions. "I made it, I made it!" shouts the top hat on the head of a nouveau-riche shark drawn by Georg Grosz; while from her balcony, a housewife spies a chimney sweep far off, stooping a little under his shabby topper. In the posters for his light-hearted films, Fred Astaire salutes us with a wave of the shiny top hat that is part of his unforgettable dance costume; meanwhile, a funeral procession passes mournfully beneath one of these posters, the coach-men hiding their bored expressions with the help of their dignified and severe top hats: All is vanity!

Within the span of the time period illustrated by the photographs in this book, the outrageous Oscar Wilde was photographed posing respectably in an equally respectable straw boater, while the mystical James Ensor painted his self-portrait wearing an outrageous straw hat decked with flowers. The soft hat with a silk grosgrain ribbon is unequivocally gangsterlike when worn by Al Capone and his pals, and the hats worn by the ne'er-do-wells in the cult movie *Borsalino* exude a suspect luxury. Yet these hats are not so very different from those favored by Humphrey Bogart for his melancholy, reserved characters, losers on the outside and winners on the inside.

Mythic Bogie: sad eyes, a trench coat, and a hat that is almost indistinguishable from the dense gray fog at the Casablanca airport–an unmistakable hat, even when Bogie appears as the worldly-wise adviser in matters erotic to the daydreaming Woody Allen in *Play It Again, Sam*.

And we can't forget the bowler: boring, arrogant, repetitive—meant to cover heads filled with clear-cut, organized ideas aimed at well-defined goals that are (for the most part) absolutely honorable. But on Charlie Chaplin's head, it's a skyrocket, a party—no matter that it's always exclusively black, it becomes a kaleidoscope of colorful ideas, a vase filled with a flower-girl's violets, a thing of hope. And so it has always been for men's hats, as though they had a life of their own, as though it were not the man who wears the hat but the hat that wears the man, in order to tell him how to be, or to seem. A real and unsettling case of *tête-à-tête*.

A Brief History of Hats

THE ANCIENT WORLD

The Italian word for hat, *cappello*, comes from the Medieval Latin *cappellu(m)*, a diminutive of the Late Latin *cappa(m)*, meaning "hood." (The English words *hat* and *hood* are of Germanic origin, but *cap* has the same root as *cappello*.) In the depths of the Middle Ages, shivering with fear and cold, no one dared to appear in public bareheaded, as had been common during the heyday of imperial Rome. Not that as private citizens, Roman men of power behaved any differently than other mortals, such as slaves, freedmen, and foreigners; like everybody else, they wore headgear to protect themselves from rain, wind, snow, and summer heat. In official artworks, however, the real "face of power" (in the elegant phrase of Sabatino Moscati), the great of Rome are always shown bareheaded, or at most veiled with a fold of the toga as in the case of Pontifex Maximus; the most glorious are shown wearing a chaplet of leaves. Caesar was the first to make a regular habit of wearing this triumphal crown, which was conferred by the Senate on victorious generals, and the other emperors all followed his lead.

Was Roman civilization, then, hatless? Officially, yes. "Virile" in the extreme (the word comes from the Latin *vir*, "man"), the Roman male was at some pains, at least in official art, to emphasize his total indifference to bad weather—unless he was shown in military uniform, in which case he wore a helmet. But the helmet belongs to the story of military headgear, and so won't be discussed here.

Despite the Romans' disdain, the wearing of hats has been well documented among many of the other people that inhabited the Italian peninsula since prehistoric times. They were worn by the Etruscans and by the colonists of Magna Graecia; inhabitants of Nuraghic-era Sardinia wore sombreros worthy of Pancho Villa; and one of the most spectacular hats in all antiquity is worn by the *Warrior of Capestrano*, a Sabine statue. This hat is quite similar to the hat made a few years ago for Signora Usuelli Borsalino from a single piece of black felt, which is included in our selection of men's hats as testimony to the continuing skill of Italian hatmakers.

*T*he Middle Ages are conventionally said to begin with the fall of the Roman Empire. The party was over: no more sumptuous palaces, heated rooms and baths, or shows of overbearing masculinity. The cowl—warm, enveloping and ending in a point—was widely worn until about the fifteenth century; when a belt was added, it became a kind of overcoat. Some men also wore caps; in Italy these were known as *berrette*, and were nothing more than removable hoods that either came to a point and hung down the back, or were flat and round. For centuries caps and hoods were the headgear for everyone, with variations due to class and fashion. High-ranking priests were allowed to wear hats; but those belong to the history of ecclesiastical headdress, not here.

In order to describe exactly where, how, and when hats were worn from the Middle Ages on would almost require an entire history of art, down to the era of the first photographs—in other words, that is yet another story. But in any event, we know that in Italy, hats were so rare and highly prized that throughout the Middle Ages only kings, princes, dukes, and counts could afford them. Generally, hats were purchased in France and, whether priced in ducats or francs, they were paid for in gold.

The hat industry truly flourished in France, and hatmakers there were officially recognized with their own guild statutes as early as 1292. In Italy, on the other hand, corporations for the makers of caps and hats were not established until 1500 in Milan and 1700 in Rome, even though colleges of craftsmen and artists of every kind had been instituted by Numa Pompilius in the eighth century B.C., according to Plutarch. By the Middle Ages, these had proliferated into dozens of universities and confraternities, guilds and companies, and would continue into the eighteenth century. In sum, there was an industry for caps and hats, but it was not vigorous enough yet to support the founding of an independent association.

THE RENAISSANCE

*I*n the fifteenth century, then, the Italian hat industry was rather unstable, as is evidenced by the absence of a hatmaking guild. Caps were still popular: at Mantua, "three thousand children and more, and as many youths" worked at producing them. Italian hats, on the other hand, could not hold their ground against Flemish competition. The highly fashionable Flemish hats invaded the market, although a Genoese regulation allowed only the sale of Italian hats made of felt, straw, and feathers. The 1500s were also a time of indecisive fashion: should one wear an extravagant hat, or a large cap in the shape of a doughnut but with a high crown, and should headgear be semi-rigid or pleated?

Yet by the first decades of the sixteenth century, the wearing of hats had become widespread, and makers of caps and hats wanted to have, if not a true guild, at least some way of organizing themselves. In Lombardy, the chief raw material for hats was wool, and the skill of the wool workers in the countryside was famous, particularly those of Monza. Wool was classified as "Venetian," or wool for extra-fine hats; "wool of Aquila," (from Abruzzi; either "tawny" or otherwise), used for medium-grade hats; or "pelizara wool," from Lombardy, for the coarsest hats. Among the most prized wools were those of Valencia and Perpignan. Other hatmakers divided hat-making wool in four groups: "Spanish Valencia" wool, Perpignan wool, Venetian wool, and "tawny wool of Ancona, and pelizara wool and wool of Bosisio." One hatmaker, Battista Bucchiero, had enough wool to produce twenty-four to thirty dozen hats a month. Another, Ambrogio Lonati, could put out "fifty hats each week." Original sources state that the extra-fine wool felt hats were tinted with wood, and that they came with or without veils, and with or without a lining of Hormuz silk (a light silk fabric, so called because originally it was shipped in from Hormuz).

The hat, often so oblivious to class distinctions, was almost as class-conscious during this period as in ancient Rome. Rich men wore hats that were "embroidered with gold, pearls, and garnets," or were "quilted, of double Hormuz silk or heavy velvet," or of wool felt. Less heavily ornamented Lombard or French felt hats were worn by the middle class, and cheap felt hats, crude and plain like "the big hats of Corteolona," were worn by the poor.

THE GUILD

$\mathcal{A}$fter many failed attempts, hatters at last established a guild, at least in Milan. The statutes were first announced by the town crier on December 4, 1568. Like other craft guilds in Monza and other towns, Milan's guild had a syndic, three consuls, and an abbot, who together constituted a kind of board of directors, a treasurer, and a notary, who kept the records of the two kinds of members: the master craftsmen (who in practice were the real operating members of the guild), and the journeymen and apprentices. The members' assembly was held on the feast of St. James, the patron saint of hatters. Both the choice of St. James as a patron and the fact that there is a St. James the Greater and a St. James the Lesser (the former being the patron in France and Milan, with a feast day celebrated on May 1, and the latter the patron in Rome and Monza, celebrated on July 25) are just two more signs of the eccentricities inherent in almost everything that has to do with hats and hatters. St. James the Lesser may have been chosen because, according to a late tradition, he was killed with a fuller's hammer by a persecutor. St. James the Greater is the patron saint of Spain and is venerated at Compostela in Galicia, a famous pilgrimage site throughout the Middle Ages. He is always shown wearing a wide wayfarer's hat. He was the brother of St. John the Evangelist, and was also a fisherman, so why did the hatters choose him as a patron? Possibly because Galicia first promoted his cult among hatters: The wool for the highest-quality hats came from Spain's Merino sheep, which were introduced by the Moors and were abundant in the pastures of Galicia, León, Segovia, and Valencia.

THE DISPUTES

$\mathcal{T}$hroughout the fifteenth and sixteenth centuries, there was no end of disputes, struggles, and difficulties among hatters, cap makers, haberdashers, and merchants, and also, particularly in Lombardy, between hatmakers in town and hatmakers in the countryside (especially around Monza and Caravaggio). Rural hatters were favored by exemptions from various taxes and by lower production costs. Severe fines and penalties—including hanging!—were specified for working without credentials or for making hats with "false" wools such as the rejects or trimmings from other hats. This latter ban was unfair, because such extra material was used not to defraud, but to make lower-grade products that anybody could afford. The thousands of obstacles, both material and moral, that the guild members set up to impede the enrollment of journeymen and apprentices, and the severe penalties imposed on the violators of the above rules and others, were truly serious attacks on the freedom of labor and commerce, but that was how the law of the most powerful operated. A harsh law, but a law nonetheless. In any event, all of this conflict made it clear that the demand for hats was constantly on the rise among all levels of the population.

*I*n Florence, a toque with a raised brim became fashionable, either plain or embellished with plumes, tufts, and ribbons. In case of rain or cold weather, the Florentines wore hats of felt or Hormuz silk. Peasants wore straw or plain cloth hats, as always. But in Turin, it was the nobility who wore straw hats—but made of "fine straw" only, of course.

In Venice the hat once again demonstrated its knack for non-conformity, independence, and contradiction: Almost everyone wore the *berretta*, except the landed gentry, who wore pointed hats of red Hormuz silk, lined with more silk or white velvet; volunteers for galley crews, who wore hats of "dark roan with a few feathers" to distinguish themselves from the convicts who served beside them; rich young men, who had "hats a yard high with backswept brims"; and peasants, who wore cheap felt hats, or on feast days, "very fine straw hats with feathers of various colors." The hat predominated over the cap in Naples; in Rome, gentlemen alternated between hats and the *berretta*.

Those Italians who imitated the French king wore wide, plumed hats with a Spanish flair, as did François I; or hats reduced to the minimum size like those of Henri II; or the silk and velvet beret brought back into style by Henri III (although when the latter toured Venice incognito, he wore a silk hat). In the time of Henri IV, the wide-brimmed plumed hat was in fashion again, but with one side of the brim turned up and the other down, in contrast to the hat worn by of François I.

Both the beginning and the end of the sixteenth century give ample proof of how hats go in and out of fashion with a logic all their own. Early in the century, for example, one of the more stylish shapes was a nearly hemispherical affair, similar to the cocked hat of the Directoire period; at the end of the century a cylindrical hat appeared that looked more like a modern top hat than would any of the hats that were worn in the next couple of centuries.

THE SEVENTEENTH CENTURY

This was the century of Spanish domination in the Duchy of Milan and in the Three Kingdoms (Naples, Sardinia, and Sicily). There was no end of intrigues in the duchies of the Po Valley, or of wars: Venice against the Turks, the Genoese against one another. It was an age of plagues, of the Counter-Reformation, of the Inquisition, and of famine brought on by taxes and shortages. As to hats, there were rebellions almost everywhere against searches and seizures of goods, and against the devastating arrests of anyone suspected of smuggling hats or attempting to evade the harsh duties of registration. As industry and commerce declined, the hatmakers' guilds became ever more strict and intolerant, to the point that sellers of "worn and used hats," or anyone in the "occupation of redyeing or mending worn hats," or foreign hatters, or hatters who were children of foreigners could be, and were, prosecuted. One had to belong to the hatters' guild even to shape a felt. In Milan, in 1643 only five authorized workshops remained of the thirty-five that had formerly provided work for more than two thousand employees.

In regard to hat styles, those who followed authentic Spanish fashion (as people did in France) wore a very large hat with the brim raised on one side and lowered on the other, usually ornamented only with a long drooping plume, similar to the hats worn by the famously pugnacious Musketeers of Louis XIII of France and his minister Richelieu. If, on the other hand, one wanted to be only a little Spanish, the hat was more modest, darker, and rounder, with a plume or two in the middle. Also fairly common were the Dutch-style hats so often painted by Rembrandt, with a low crown and a wide brim and plumes, or with a tall crown and a wide, flat brim, as for example in the portrait, not of the hatters' guild, but of the *Syndics of the Drapers' Guild*.

The seventeenth century was not a happy one. It was the time of Don Abbondio, the Innominato, a character in Manzoni's classic novel *I promessi sposi*; of hired thugs; and of the persecution of Galileo by the Inquisition. In Italy it was a century of high drama, not favorable for the hat, whose essence always seems to contain a measure of joyous foolishness.

In France, the showy hats favored at the start of the century by Louis XIII gave way to the colossal curled wigs of Louis XIV, the Sun

King. The hat that interfered least with the wig was the tricorne, which was all the more desirable because it could be festooned with plumes, ornaments, tassels, and braid, becoming so overloaded that it usually was carried under the arm and not worn on the head, again in order not to disturb the wig.

THE EIGHTEENTH CENTURY

*E*arly in the 1700s, it seemed as though the hat industry would never prosper. In Milan, to escape taxes and other vexations the only remedy was to leave for the provinces, which meant Monza, so that in 1713 the hatmakers' guild had a total enrollment of fourteen people. To correct the situation, in 1710 Prince Eugene of Savoy proclaimed a ban on the importation into Milan, even from the nearby countryside, of "all kinds of foreign felt hats," except those made entirely or partly of beaver, or "cheap, hairy hats to be worn by the poor." These exceptions were essential: the latter to avoid antagonizing the populace, and the former to avoid undermining the few surviving purveyors to the dandies who followed the fashion for beaver hats.

The beaver-hat craze had exploded in England and from there had spread throughout Europe and even to South America. In France, La Rochelle was a production and distribution center for beaver-fur felt. The pelts were brought from Canada by way of Russia, and made into hats that were *"doux, luisants et à poil"* (soft, shimmering, and made of fur) and almost endlessly recyclable. Handed down from master to servant, then sold back to La Rochelle, they were restored with a coat of glue, then resold in Spain and Portugal, where the style was for stiff hats with either a short nap or no nap at all. Worn out once again, the very same hats were reconditioned and shipped off this time to Brazil, where the young rich people favored hats that were "flabby, with a snap edge."

La Rochelle declined after the revocation of the Edict of Nantes: 300,000 Protestant subjects, including almost all the hatters in La Rochelle, fled the country. In Brandenburg, the exiles taught their craft to the Germans. In England, in 1760 alone the Hudson Bay Company brought back enough pelts from America for 576,000 beaver hats, showing just how popular this fur had become.

In Italy, on the other hand, as we learn from petitions for tax exemptions on not just wool but other processing materials (soap, oils, dyes, and chemicals), hatters chiefly used "hair of camel, rabbit, vicuña wool, silk, floss-silk, linen, and cotton." In Milan, as everywhere else, people still wore the tricorne. But new times were knocking at the door: It was the Age of Enlightenment.

THE SILK HAT

*B*y now, no one wore the Italian caps called *berrette*, but the shiny elegance of their silk had not been forgotten. The first producer of silk hats, the probable forerunners of the top hat that would officially be born in 1796, was the Parisian Leprevost. Though personally assailed by the guilds, he opened the way for a revival of the French hat industry. The same thing happened in Milan to the enterprising Giovanni Battista Gnecchi, who had been making "fine hats, including beaver" at Melegnano for twenty years. He moved to Milan and won a succession of the fat gold prize purses of the Società Patriottica, which not only gave him prestige but, above all, the means to double his production.

The money also enabled Gnecchi to improve the shine and color of his silk hats. Gnecchi was an unsurpassed master of color; his two-toned fur hats made of pure hare fur variously combined blue, green, ash-gray, brown, and black. He invented hats made of one-third white silk plus beaver. Supported even by the famous jurist and philosopher Cesare Beccaria, in 1789 Gnecchi had a factory and shop in Milan, at Santa Radegonda. Finally, he achieved his own small revolution: He made the transition from floss silk to true spun silk.

Gnecchi's was the first company in Italy to operate in a modern way, systematically subdividing and specializing labor, planning, and distribution. According to an estimate made for Eugene of Savoy, 193 hats were produced in Milan in 1716. In 1789, Gnecchi made 3,379, and projected 6,500 for the next year.

THE NINETEENTH CENTURY

With the nineteenth century dawned the golden age of the top hat. Once a revolutionary symbol, this hat soon evolved into the hat of the elite. In the early days of the century, top hats were made of beaver, and only the upper classes could afford them. They replaced the old-fashioned bicorne, a carryover from the preceding century, as the proper hat for evening wear. By 1840, however, they had exploded in popularity and were donned by men of all walks of life, becoming the typical hat for daytime use. The driving force behind the fashion was a change in materials: thanks to an Italian method developed in the late eighteenth century, top hats started to appear in silk "hatter's plush" instead of beaver, bringing down the price and making the top hat available to the masses. Even the poorest man could afford the second-hand hats that were now widely sold, silk hats being easier to repair and salvage than delicate beaver ones. Now everyone could dress like a gentleman, and top hats were seen on construction workers at building sites, on policemen walking their beats, even on shepherds grazing their flocks.

Despite protests from progressives, who favored soft, round felt hats inspired by artists, the top hat continued to dominate men's fashion throughout the 1850s and '60s. It grew increasingly taller and narrower, becoming so unwieldy that collapsible versions that could fit into one's pocket were soon flourishing. It is perhaps due to this inconvenience of the tall top hat that new, informal hat styles began to make their mark toward the end of the century.

Although the top hat was worn in all ranks of society, it never lost its veneer of nobility, and this was the reason for the protest against it in liberal circles. The new hats springing up were truly democratic in origin and were necessitated by the increase in leisure time and recreational activity. Two favorites were the straw hat, favored by sailors the world over and seen as a typically American hat, common in the South; and the derby, a stiff felt hat similar in shape to the round artists' hat often seen at the seaside starting in the mid-nineteenth century. The derby, also called the bowler, was considered to be much more convenient than the top hat, although it did grow in height as the decades passed. By the 1880s it was firmly established as the "best hat" of the working classes, while a wide variety of casual headgear became available—from the "Alpine" hat, precursor to the fedora, and hats of tropical origin, such as the panama from Central America, to caps inspired by military styles.

Despite the outcry of the progressives over the "elitist" top hat, it was in retrospect a more democratic trend than any of the later "populist" hats. During its heyday, the top hat was worn by every man, regardless of his station in life. By the end of the century, hats were once again an index to social class, the working man preferring the bowler, while the noble and professional classes tended to cling to the top hat. All this changed in our century, however, when the hat became, above all, a political symbol.

THE TWENTIETH CENTURY

The twentieth century contributed no new styles to men's wardrobes, but rather continued to build upon old styles. Just as the lounge suit replaced the formal frock coat early in the century, the informal hat came to dominate men's fashions. Over the course of years, the top hat faded into the background, reserved only for formal occasions; the bowler took on the elitist image that the top hat had once carried. The homburg replaced the bowler as the average man's semiformal hat, and the casual hat enjoyed great success. By the twenties, it had become fashionable to look as if you were on vacation year-round. The straw boater was all the rage early in the century, and linen and tweed sports hats were seen in the city as well as in the country.

The trilby, first seen in the previous century, was reintroduced just after World War I in a lighter, more comfortable version that fit the faster pace of life in the modern era. An exaggerated version with pointy top and wide brims, made by Borsellino, is still remembered as the trademark hat of the gangster. The extraordinary popularity of the trilby cast a shadow over all other kinds of hat, which were further endangered by the shortage of hatmaking supplies during World War II. The black silk top hat had to be replaced by one of gray felt, and the shortage of shellac nearly wiped out the bowler, though it did reemerge after the war. Generally speaking, however, the men's hatmaking industry did not recover, with hatlessness becoming a growing trend. Throughout the fifties, the hatmaking industry tried introducing new forms and styles, but various fads emerged only to die out again.

By the 1960s, hats had become so rare that they were taken up by avant-garde artists who wanted to make a splash. The Beatles made their short-peaked black caps popular for a while, but by their time, young men generally went bareheaded. Today one occasionally sees a top hat on a formally dressed man, but the bowler no longer graces the head of the average businessman. In America at least, the baseball cap comes closest to playing the role the top hat once did. Hatlessness, once considered to be verging on indecency, is now the rule. After so many centuries we have returned to the Roman way. But as fashion goes in cycles, so we may not have seen the last of the hat. With the growing interest in vintage clothing, second-hand trilbies and other dress hats are increasingly seen on young people's heads—who can say what time will bring?

Acknowledgments

The author and the publisher would like to thank Mayor Giuseppe Mirabelli, Alderman Giulio Massobrio, Dr. Mario Bruno, Signora Usuelli Borsalino, and Signora Castellaro for their kind collaboration and for permitting access to the collection and archives of the Hat Museum in Alessandria.

For providing access to the collection and archives of the Monza and Brianza Ethnological Museum, we would like to thank in particular President Sorteni, Dr. Giacovelli, and Dr. Massarotti. Our thanks also to Signore Maurizio Mutinelli.

Bella Cosa